REZ CHEESE 2

ELIZABETH WILEY MA JD, POMO ELDER

Order this book online at www.trafford.com
or email orders@trafford.com

Most Trafford titles are also available at major online book retailers.

 www.trafford.com

North America & international
toll-free: 844 688 6899 (USA & Canada)
fax: 812 355 4082

Our mission is to efficiently provide the world's finest, most comprehensive book publishing service, enabling every author to experience success. To find out how to publish your book, your way, and have it available worldwide, visit us online at www.trafford.com

ISBN: 978-1-6987-1032-7 (sc)
      978-1-6987-1031-0 (e)

Print information available on the last page.

Trafford rev. 11/17/2021

REZ CHEESE 2

Native Americans, and other Native cultures living in two cultures without drugs, suicide, or poverty

1st Edition

Introduction: Rez Cheese, a book about many thoughts. Mainly started from the thought of the huge blocks of mostly cheap left over military surplus cheese sent to the reserves to meet the treaty mandates to provide food to the Natives in exchange for stopping the fighting for their own land.

Rez Cheese 2 is a book that while including more recipes that will lead Natives to explore their own Native foods, and how to buy or grow them as needed since most of the food protected and exchanged in the "old" days is now dead, extinct, and/or polluted out of existence by mining, factories, and dumping of toxic waste in ground water supplies, or lakes and oceans.

Rez Cheese 2 is about helping out youth to become inspired by our stories, NOT ridden with bitterness and anger (the author well knows those feelings as explained in the book).

Rez Cheese 2 is about all Native Nations people inspiring others to salvage, restore and reclaim the earth, air, water, and even the DIRT (yes that is a science career today, to restore DIRT for restoration of forests, prairies, marshlands, and farming).

Rez Cheese 2 is about not giving up. We have many inspirational people in our heritage, both local nations, and across the Americas. Suicide, drug addiction, sex trafficking and addiction to pornography are NOT our ways, they demean a person's soul and the person dies, or kills themselves.

Our traditions tell us our Creator gave us each a duty, to protect nature, the animals, and each other to make the world better for the next seven generations, and to teach thee young people to do the same. Look forward with hope, not backward with anger and bitterness. We all know what happens to people who move looking backwards, instead of where they are going.

ELDERS: teach your children to respect them, teach elders to be respectable.

OUR culture teaches that we ALL respect our Elders, yet those Elders MUST learn to be respectable since many have spent their lives away from OUR culture. A drunken, addicted thief, or couch potato is NOT what is meant by an elder that has earned respect. BUT, our culture says, just because they are O L D we must respect them enough to make sure they have safe housing, healthy food, and a listen to give us wisdom in our prayers for these elders that have been broken by not being raised in our ways and support of their own nation.

During law school, I made many trips out into the farthest reaches of reservations and talked to the elders at the curb an Native Nations centers (I personally do NOT use thee word tribe, it is demeaning, meant to denote the uneducated, unnecessary people waiting for the great civilized to come and rescue them from centuries of harmony with nature, and living in peace within confederacies that existed from the top of Alaska to the tip of S. America to let people live, travel and trade in peace and protect nature and the animals for the next seven generations. I generally found a teen, or young adult that could speak American and their own Native language to come and translate for me.

As a child, many of my relatives, rebelling against the BIA and Catholic schools they were rounded up and forced to attend, had become ministers in Assembly of God churches and went all over the nations teaching that Jesus helped us all to forgive, and to return to OUR culture and honor, as well as how to be our own best people to glorify our Creator. These "tent" or "revival" meetings that our family went to support our relatives taught me a lot, and opened doors that were not open to many other scholars and/or researchers. When I went to college and then law school, I went back and asked, how did the traditional laws work? There is a really good documentary on PBS from a Stanford study of some Native Nations formal legal systems. Native America is the title.

My Mother had attended UCLA and Berkeley, she occasionally brought researchers to meet old, ancient elders, supposedly to learn from them. My Dad's Great Uncle was the last of our real healers, when he spoke to some of the researchers he told them of beheading wild game hens, and all kinds of things my father, who was translating, had never, never seen. My

Dad asked him why he had done that after the researchers left. He said he felt that they did NOT want to hear what he had learned and had to say, they wanted him to tell them what they wanted to believe and write about the Native Nations humans who managed for at least three thousand years to keep a balance with nature and protect the animals, fish and birds, as well as each other before the land barons, and the gold rush put them in the way of bounty hunters and genocidal troops that in the past year the Governor has researched and formally apologized for the illegal creation of genocide bills, and paying for it by taxpayer dollars.

PROGRAM SERIES INTRODUCTION:

INTRODUCTION:

Our books are written as on ongoing series for high risk youth, veterans, and first responders as well as their parents and those who are raising them.

One of the reasons for starting this series was we, as special needs teachers, as therapists, as Directors of programs and private schools for high risk youth began to recognize how many of the children and youth were children of veterans, grandchildren of veterans, and also first responders.

We then noticed the numbers of minority children and poverty level financial back grounds were the reality for high risk children and youth. We saw children of Mothers who had been as young as NINE at the birth of their child among the high risk students. Whether rich, or poverty level, we saw children of alcohol, sexual, and drug addictions.

We saw children as young as 18 months labeled with an alphabet of mental health disorders, medicated and put into "special schools" where in fact media found they were often warehoused, abused, and not taught at all. Upon seeing a news story about the schools discovered at some of the licensed sites, in which children and teens often did not have desks, or chairs to sit on, let alone proper educational supplies and equipment for special learning program, we joined with others, and designed programs.

We were naive enough to think our work, offered FREE in most cases, would be welcomed especially as we offer it free and often through research projects, but, it was NOT valued or wanted.

What? we asked?

We went back to college and while earning degrees we had apparently NOT needed while working with children of the very rich in expensive private schools, we did research projects to document our findings. To find ways to overcome the problems. Again, our work was NOT valued or wanted.

One of our associates, who had asked many of us to volunteer in a once a month FREE reading program in the local public schools, was held back for almost two years doing paperwork and proving her volunteers, most of them parents of successful children, teens and adults, could read a first five years book and teach parents how to read those books to their own children. She was a Deputy United States Prosecutor, and had recruited friends from all levels of law enforcement, child and family services, education and volunteer groups that served children and families.

None the less, we continued our work, met a fabulous and expensive Psychiatrist who was building his own server system and the first online education project after creating a massive and encompassing medical examination study guide for graduate medical students to assist them in passing global and national medical examinations for licensing.

We worked with a team of citizens and specialists in education who had created a 39 manual project for students, parents and teachers to be able to learn on their own.

This series of books includes ideas, history and thoughts from the students, the parents, and professionals who work with these situations.

Jesus was told, don't have children wasting your time, and he responded, let the children come.

Our work is to bring children to us, and to those who have the heart and love to develop the uniqueness and individuality of each of God's creations. Many of them are of different religions, and beliefs, and many are atheists but believe fully in the wonder and uniqueness of every human.

To all who have helped and continue to help children and anyone wanting to learn, we thank God and we thank you.

Chapter One

Elders

List the Elders in your life:

These Elders do NOT have to be from your own Native Nation.

Almost all, if not all, Native Nations do not believe in incest, and include incest to second cousins. One of the divisions CONGRESS put on Native Nations is to make a person decide to only be ONE Nation citizen. While it makes sense that a person should not be allowed to take benefits from both Nations, while others in both nations go without. In the days before contact and genocide, the Native Nations had specific laws concerning which Nation a person was a citizen to, many times it was the Mother's family Nation that determined the Nation of the children. After the reservations and Congress became involved census and treaty rights membership became the legal citizenship criteria. Children were always considered "family" to all nations they were related to by blood, for one reason, they had to be sure not to marry first or second cousins from the other nations.

List your Elders, and those who by age you need to respect. This does NOT mean you have to do what they say, it does mean you have to listen respectfully to what they say to you. In many Native Nations I studies during the sixties and seventies, a "youngster" was considered anyone under thirty five or so. In community meetings, if a person under thirty five, except possibly soldiers and protectors of "the people" asked an Elder to present their feelings, or suggestions to the council. BUT children and teens, and young adults were expected to attend meetings in silence and pay respect to the discussions, even if they went on for days.

List things you have done to disrespect your Elders and the Elders of your Nation. Talk to Elders in your family and Nation to find out the ways to formally apologize and to make up to those you have offended. Keep in mind that Native Nations generally felt actions that gave humiliation to the ancestors were still disrespect to those Elders long passed.

Chapter Two

NO MORE SUICIDE

Suicide has to stop. In our Elders, mid range adults, and in teens and children.

ASK the Elders for help with your problems.

Join groups, or create groups of people your age to join together and with joy figure out how to do each of our duty to ourselves, others, and nature and the animals.

Addictions and unsafe behaviors are just a different form of suicide.

LIST all ways to get help for yourself and others you know at risk for suicide. Our traditions do NOT have lists of bad things that make any of us useless and bad....Our traditions ask us to ask the Elders and Healers to help us cleanse. A lot of nations are going back to special sweat lodges for men, and for women to address many issues together.

Chapter Three

ENDING ADDICTIONS

People think drinking and drugs are addictions. THEY ARE. But gossiping, over eating, not taking care of your health, not exercising, or over exercising, bad driving, not working, not making your dreams come true by YOUR work, instead of laying around being sad because the dream fairy did not give you everything you wanted, ALL are addictions.

What addictions to YOU have. What groups or programs are there to help you. Creator created each of us uniquely, perfectly, and we have learned from racial hate, genocide and our own look at commercials, movies, and others to think we are NOT OK and use drugs, drinking or other addictions to stop the pain.

Chapter Four

EDUCATION: Our Way

Bicultural Development. Seriously, being someones MAID, or the type of nurse that whoopty doo, gets to clean dirty rear ends, NEVER the RN's and top techs, or administrators is NOT the dreams of the Nations First Citizens.

We can choose to learn HOW to be prepared for the higher education to get the jobs that can help others, and integrate our own forms of medication and healing into more current healthcare for the best of all those we care for.

We can choose to learn HOW to be prepared for the sciences to clean up and restore the environment and to build housing and cities in both cultures.

We can choose to learn HOW to use our own forms of art, dance, music and healing to help everyone heal from centuries of hate and division not just in America, or the Americas, but globally as we network with good people everywhere.

ART, our way

Art in the money culture. Do be an artist, even it you just make something you enjoy making and have to work a "job" to pay the bills, DO NOT BE a Fartist, a drugged, up, drunk trend follower who THINKS you are all that and sliced bread as well.

Drama

Learning that "our" drama is equal to any other form of dramatic arts. Respect your own culture, and do NOT let weird drug taking rich kids steal it away by wearing leather and feathers.

Music, Poetry, Songs

Have you had someone tell you that you are not a Native artist because you play classic piano, or guitar, or can act, or been called "exotic" because you are not the usual commercial ad person........or because you think drums might be a set of drums in a band, not JUST a pow wow drum.....it is time to stand up for your own art.

List local and national art, drama and music groups that will help us ALL to heal, and to share our talents. Whether one batch of fry bread tacos at a special holiday meal once a year for the community center, or one pair of earrings to auction off to fundraise for community programs and scholarships for our own local Native Nation students, share your art, music, write plays, screenplays, Our traditions say share your art, because it is you, and not to make money. It might be that you can make money at the same time, or maybe have a job that will support you to create your one or two amazing offerings a year, or in a lifetime.

Chapter Eight

Clothing

Most of the world's people wear tee shirts, with something drawn or written on them that means something to the wearer, and jeans, or shorts and bare feet, flip flops, or sandals, or tennis shoes. Be proud of who YOU are, do NOT try and be someone else, and for God's sake, do NOT wear someone else's name on your butt to make you think you are OK.

Chapter Nine

Car, other vehicles, and safety

Pick your right foot up in the air, press down the toe, as far as you can. THAT is it. Driving fast in an old unsafe car, or drunk, on drugs, or racing on public streets is NOT cool, it is not OK, it is just stupid. If you think all those people you cut off are saying "wowsie, what a great driver" they are not, and that finger they have raised is NOT some ancient sign of adoration.

Chapter Ten

BE SAFE

Across America, and from the top of Alaska, to the southern most tip of S. America and all the islands between still have people who believe in the goodness of others. It has caused a lot of maiming, torture, sex trafficking and death to our people.

BE SAFE. Learn to stay with those you know to be safe. Learn to stay where the evil people can not grab you.

Learn not to do "trendy" things that lead you and many times your family, and your children into unsafe conditions.

List things that you do that may be too trusting, or not careful enough. How can you cage those things.

Chapter Eleven

LEARNING to succeed or survive in the dominant money culture, but choose your own individual lifestyle.

How to balance your life with what commercials and talk shows tell you SHOULD be.

List things from the dominant money culture that you think you want. Find classes and books that teach you how to get them with sense. Your own Rez credit union may have credit building programs to help you. First time buyer programs and education savings programs to help both you and your children meet your dreams.

Chapter Twelve

Closing:

This book is offered as a push to each Native American, Native across the globe, to learn how to put aside the bitterness and anger of the genocides, and stealing of our lands and cultures. To know that not ALL people of any culture or race are guilty of what others of their culture or race have done in the past, or do today.

Each of us needs to do what in the past were often called vision quests. Time out, in quiet, *a west or meditation period with the help of Elders and healers to set a course for your life to give you happiness and joy, while you meet your duties to your family, your children, and the animals and nature, to the next seven generations. Without humiliation, or feeling bullied and put down by the great 'athey". Find your way. Find our Creator to give you strength. Find others in your same boat and row with them on this voyage of ours.*

24

Other books in our programs:

Closing and Other Books by Author and team

Closing:

All of our group of books, and workbooks contain some work pages, and/or suggestions for the reader, and those teaching these books to make notes, to go to computer, and libraries and ask others for information to help these projects work their best.

To utilize these to their fullest, make sure YOU model the increased thoughts and availability of more knowledge to anyone you share these books and workbooks with in classes, or community groups.

Magazines are, as noted in most of the books, a wonderful place to look for and find ongoing research and information. Online search engines often bring up new research in the areas, and newly published material.

We all have examples of how we learned and who it was that taught us.

One of the strangest lessons I have learned was walking to a shoot in downtown Los Angeles. The person who kindly told me to park my truck in

Pasadena, and take the train had been unaware that the weekend busses did NOT run early in the morning when the crews had to be in to set up. That person, being just a participant, was going much later in the day, taking a taxi, and had no idea how often crews do NOT carry purses with credit cards, large amounts of cash, and have nowhere to carry those items, because the crew works hard, and fast during a set up and tear down and after the shoot are TIRED and not looking to have to find items that have been left around, or stolen.

As I walked, I had to travel through an area of Los Angeles that had become truly run down and many homeless were encamped about and sleeping on the sidewalks and in alleys. I saw a man, that having worked in an ER for many years I realized was DEAD. I used to have thoughts about people who did not notice people needing help, I thought, this poor man, this is probably the most peace he has had in a long time. I prayed for him and went off to my unwanted walk across town. As I walked, I thought about myself, was I just heartless, or was I truly thinking this was the only moment of peace this man had had for a long time and just leaving him to it. What good were upset neighbors, and police, fire trucks and ambulances going to do. He was calmly, eyes open, staring out at a world that had failed him while alive, why rush to disturb him now that nothing could be done.

I did make sure he was DEAD. He was, quite cold rigid.

I learned that day that it is best to do what a person needs, NOT what we need.

Learning is about introspection and grounding of material. Passing little tests on short term memory skills and not knowing what it all means is NOT education, or teaching.

As a high school student, in accelerated Math and Science programs, in which I received 4.0

grades consistently, I walked across a field, diagonally, and suddenly all that math and science made sense, it was not just exercises on paper I could throw answers back on paper, but I realized had NO clue as to what it all really meant.

OTHER BOOKS by this author, and team

Most, if not all, of these books are written at a fourth grade level. FIrst, the author is severely brain damaged from a high fever disease caused by a sample that came in the mail, without a warning that it had killed during test marketing. During the law suit, it was discovered that the corporation had known prior to mailing out ten million samples, WITHOUT warnings of disease and known deaths, and then NOT telling anyone after a large number of deaths around the world started. Second, the target audience is high risk youth, and young veterans, most with a poor education before signing into, or being drafted into the military as a hope Many of our veterans are Vietnam or WWII era.

Maybe those recruiting promises would come true. They would be trained, educated, and given chance for a home, and to protect our country and its principles. Watch the movies Platoon, and Born on the Fourth of July as well as the Oliver Stone series on history to find out how these dreams were meet.

DO NOT bother to write and tell us of grammar or spelling errors. We often wrote these books and workbooks fast for copyrights. We had learned our lessons about giving our material away when one huge charity asked us for our material, promising a grant, Instead, we heard a couple of years later they had built their own VERY similar project, except theirs charged for services, ours were FREE, and theirs was just for a small group, ours was training veterans and others to spread the programs as fast as they could.. They got a Nobel Peace prize. We keep saying we are not bitter, we keep saying we did not do our work to get awards, or thousands of dollars of grants....but, it hurts. Especially when lied to and that group STILL sends people to US for help when they can not meet the needs, or the veterans and family can not afford their "charitable" services. One other group had the nerve to send us a Cease and Desist using our own name. We said go ahead and sue, we have proof of legal use of this name for decades. That man had the conscience to apologize, his program was not even FOR veterans or first responders, or their families, nor high risk kids. But we learned. Sometimes life is very unfair.

We got sued again later for the same issue. We settled out of Court as our programs were just restarting and one of the veterans said, let's just change that part of the name and keep on training veterans to run their own programs. Smart young man.

Book List:

DRAGON KITES and other stories:

The Grandparents Story list will add 12 new titles this year. We encourage every family to write their own historic stories. That strange old Aunt who when you listen to her stories left a rich and well regulated life in the Eastern New York coastal fashionable families to learn Telegraph messaging and go out to the old west to LIVE her life. That old Grandfather or Grandmother who was sent by family in other countries torn by war to pick up those "dollars in the streets" as noted in the book of that title.

Books in publication, or out by summer 2021

Carousel Horse: A Children's book about equine therapy and what schools MIGHT be and are in special private programs.

Carousel Horse: A smaller version of the original Carousel Horse, both contain the workbooks and the screenplays used for on site stable programs as well as lock down programs where the children and teens are not able to go out to the stables.

Spirit Horse II: This is the work book for training veterans and others interested in starting their own Equine Therapy based programs. To be used as primary education sites, or for supplementing public or private school programs. One major goal of this book is to copyright our founding material, as we gave it away freely to those who said they wanted to help us get grants. They did not. Instead they built their own programs, with grant money, and with donations in small, beautiful stables and won....a Nobel Peace Prize for programs we invented. We learned our lessons, although we do not do our work for awards, or grants, we DO not like to be ripped off, so now we copyright.

Reassessing and Restructuring Public Agencies; This book is an over view of our government systems and how they were expected to be utilized for public betterment. This is a Fourth Grade level condemnation of a PhD dissertation that was not accepted be because the mentor thought it was "against government" .. The first paragraph noted that a request had been made, and referrals given by the then White House.

Reassessing and Restructuring Public Agencies; TWO. This book is a suggestive and creative work to give THE PEOPLE the idea of taking back their government and making the money spent and the agencies running SERVE the PEOPLE ;not politicians. This is NOT against government, it is about the DUTY of the PEOPLE to oversee and control government before it overcomes us.

Could This Be Magic? A Very Short Book. This is a very short book of pictures and the author's personal experiences as the Hall of Fame band VAN HALEN practiced in her garage. The pictures are taken by the author, and her then five year old son. People wanted copies of the pictures, and permission was given to publish them to raise money for treatment and long term Veteran homes.

Carousel TWO: Equine therapy for Veterans. publication pending 2021

Carousel THREE: Still Spinning: Special Equine therapy for women veterans and single mothers. This book includes TWELVE STEPS BACK FROM BETRAYAL for soldiers who have been sexually assaulted in the active duty military and help from each other to heal, no matter how horrible the situation. publication pending 2021

LEGAL ETHICS: AN OXYMORON. A book to give to lawyers and judges you feel have not gotten the justice of American Constitution based law (Politicians are great persons to gift with this book). Publication late 2021

PARENTS CAN LIVE and raise great kids.

Included in this book are excerpts from our workbooks from KIDS ANONYMOUS and KIDS JR, and A PARENTS PLAIN RAP (to teach sexuality and relationships to their children. This program came from a copyrighted project thirty years ago, which has been networked into our other programs. This is our training work book. We asked AA what we had to do to become a real Twelve Step program as this is considered a quasi twelve step program children and teens can use to heal BEFORE becoming involved in drugs, sexual addiction, sexual trafficking and relationship woes, as well as unwanted, neglected and abused or having children murdered by parents not able to deal with the reality of parenting. Many of our original students were children of abuse and neglect, no matter how wealthy. Often the neglect was by society itself when children lost parents to illness, accidents or addiction. We were told, send us a copy and make sure you call it quasi. The Teens in the first programs when surveyed for the outcome research reports said, WE NEEDED THIS EARLIER. SO they helped younger children invent KIDS JR. Will be republished in 2021 as a documentary of the work and success of these projects.

Addicted To Dick. This is a quasi Twelve Step program for women in domestic violence programs mandated by Courts due to repeated incidents and danger, or actual injury or death of their children.

Addicted to Dick 2018 This book is a specially requested workbook for women in custody, or out on probation for abuse to their children, either by themselves or their sexual partners or spouses. The estimated national number for children at risk at the time of request was three million across the nation. During Covid it is estimated that number has risen. Homelessness and undocumented families that are unlikely to be reported or found are creating discussion of a much larger number of children maimed or killed in these domestic violence crimes. THE most important point in this book is to force every local school district to train teachers, and all staff to recognize children at risk, and to report their family for HELP, not punishment. The second most important part is to teach every child on American soil to know to ask for help, no matter that parents, or other relatives or known adults, or unknown adults have threatened to kill them for "telling". Most, if not all paramedics, emergency rooms, and police and fire stations are trained to protect the children and teens, and get help for the family.. PUNISHMENT is not the goal, eliminating childhood abuse and injury or death at the hands of family is the goal of all these projects. In some areas JUDGES of child and family courts were taking training and teaching programs themselves to HELP. FREE..

Addicted to Locker Room BS. This book is about MEN who are addicted to the lies told in locker rooms and bars. During volunteer work at just one of several huge juvenile lock downs, where juveniles who have been convicted as adults, but are waiting for their 18th birthday to be sent to adult prisons, we noticed that the young boys and teens had "big" ideas of themselves, learned in locker rooms and back alleys. Hundreds of these young boys would march, monotonously around the enclosures, their lives over. often facing long term adult prison sentences.

The girls, we noticed that the girls, for the most part were smart, had done well in school, then "something" happened. During the years involved in this volunteer work I saw only ONE young girl who was so mentally ill I felt she was not reachable, and should be in a locked down mental health facility for help; if at all possible, and if teachers, and others had been properly trained, helped BEFORE she gotten to that place, lost in the horror and broken of her childhood and early teen years.

We noticed that many of the young women in non military sexual assault healing programs were "betrayed" in many ways, by step fathers, boyfriends, even fathers, and mothers by either molestation by family members, or allowing family members or friends of parents to molest these young women, often as small children. We asked military sexually assaulted young women to begin to volunteer to help in the programs to heal the young girls and teens, it helped heal them all.

There was NOTHING for the boys that even began to reach them until our research began on the locker room BS theory of life destruction and possible salvaging by the boys themselves, and men in prisons who helped put together something they thought they MIGHT have heard before they ended up in prison.

Americans CAN Live Happily Ever After. Parents edition.One

Americans CAN Live Happily Ever After. Children's edition Two.

Americans CAN Live Happily Ever After. Three. After Covid. This book includes "Welcome to America" a requested consult workbook for children and youth finding themselves in cages, auditoriums on cots, or in foster group homes or foster care of relatives or non-relatives with NO guidelines for their particular issues. WE ASKED the kids, and they helped us write this fourth grade level workbook portion of this book to help one another and each other. Written in a hurry! We were asked to use our expertise in other youth programs, and our years of experience teaching and working in high risk youth programs to find something to help.

REZ CHEESE Written by a Native American / WASP mix woman. Using food, and thoughts on not getting THE DIABETES, stories are included of a childhood between two worlds.

REZ CHEESE TWO A continuation of the stress on THE DIABETES needing treatment and health care from birth as well as recipes, and stories from Native America, including thoughts on asking youth to help stop the overwhelming numbers of suicide by our people.

BIG LIZ: LEADER OF THE GANG Stories of unique Racial Tension and Gang Abatement projects created when gangs and racial problems began to make schools unsafe for our children.

DOLLARS IN THE STREETS, ghost edited for author Lydia Caceras, the first woman horse trainer at Belmont Park.

95 YEARS of TEACHING:

A book on teaching, as opposed to kid flipping

Two teachers who have created and implemented systems for private and public education a combined 95 plus years of teaching talk about experiences and realities and how parents can get involved in education for their children. Included are excerpts from our KIDS

ANONYMOUS and KIDS JR workbooks of over 30 years of free youth programs.

A HORSE IS NOT A BICYCLE. A book about pet ownership and how to prepare your children for responsible pet ownership and along the way to be responsible parents. NO ONE needs to own a pet, or have a child, but if they make that choice, the animal, or child deserves a solid, caring forever home.

OLD MAN THINGS and MARE'S TALES. this is a fun book about old horse trainers I met along the way. My husband used to call the old man stories "old man things", which are those enchanting and often very effective methods of horse, pet, and even child rearing. I always said I brought up my children and my students the same as I had trained horses and dogs......I meant that horses and dogs had taught me a lot of sensible, humane ways to bring up an individual, caring, and dream realizing adult who was HAPPY and loved.

STOP TALKING, DO IT

ALL of us have dreams, intentions, make promises. This book is a workbook from one of our programs to help a person make their dreams come true, to build their intentions into goals, and realities, and to keep their promises. One story from this book, that inspired the concept is a high school kid, now in his sixties, that was in a special ed program for drug abuse and not doing well in school. When asked, he said his problem was that his parents would not allow him to buy a motorcycle. He admitted that he did not have money to buy one, insure one, take proper driver's education and licensing examinations to own one, even though he had a job. He was asked to figure out how much money he was spending on drugs. Wasting his own money, stealing from his parents and other relatives, and then to figure out, if he saved his own money, did some side jobs for neighbors and family until he was 18, he COULD afford the motorcycle and all it required to legally own one. In fact, he did all, but decided to spend the money on college instead of the motorcycle when he graduated from high school. His priorities had changed as he learned about responsible motorcycle ownership and risk doing the assignments needed for his special ed program. He also gave up drugs, since his stated reason was he could not have a motorcycle, and that was no longer true, he COULD have a motorcycle, just had to buy it himself, not just expect his parents to give it to him.

Printed in the United States
by Baker & Taylor Publisher Services